Coton Eskin
20 Milestone Cha

C000113206

Coton Eskimo Memorable Moments. Includes Milestones for Memories, Gifts, Socialization & Training

Volume 1

Todays Doggy

Copyright © 2019

Dedicated To All of You Wonderful Owners and Fans

Introduction

Welcome to the Original Doggy Milestone Series™ where you are encouraged to create those special moments with your dog. We have composed the milestones in a way that challenges you to set the stage before taking your photos.

Use props and make it fun - be creative in setting up your photos. Get family and friends involved - take it out with you - use it in different places and settings - have a play with it and most importantly, have a good time!

You can either hold the desired milestone spread open yourself - or have somebody hold it open as you take the snap.

If you would like to have the selected milestone book spread open and standing independently in your photos, you can use one or two large 'foldback' clips to hold the spread open.

Good luck and enjoy your photo fun.

I Love My My Family...

...And My Family Loves Me

At The
Beach!

Having a **Wave** of a **Time**

With My Doggy Pals

IT'S...

BED
TIME

I DIDN'T KNOW WHICH STICK YOU THREW

SO I BOUGHT BACK ALL OF THEM

They Say Diamonds Are a Girl's Best Friend

I Disagree! I'm The Only "Best Friend" Here!

I'm Going To Start Eating Healthy...

Next Week!

PLAYING IN THE LEAVES

I Need

a

HUGe

Amount
Of
Treats

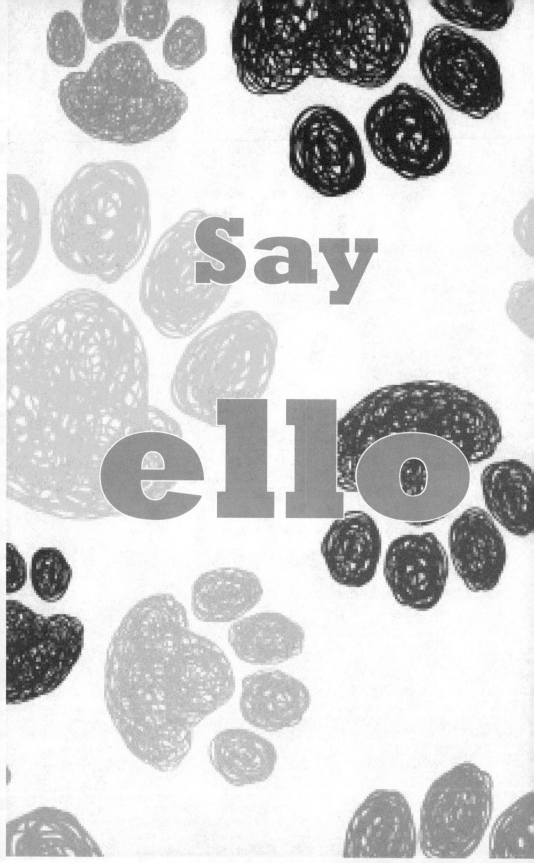

To My Little Friend

OFF

To

The

VET??

CATCH ME IF YOU CAN!

KEEP

CALM

WE'RE A TEAM

NASA

Wants

To Hire

Me

Because

I'm a

STAR!

OOPS!
I
Buried
Your
Stuff

...But I
Forgot
Where

I'm a Super Hero

My Real Name Is SUPER POOCH

Very

Incredible

Pup

I

DIDN'T

DO IT

I'll Just Be Over Here...

Looking

Fabulous

PLEASE

PLEASE

PRETTY PLEEEASE

CAN I KEEP IT?

I'm On a SEAFOOD Diet

CPSIA information can be obtained
at www.ICGtesting.com
Printed in the USA
LVHW080604200819
628164LV00009B/1019/P

9 781395 324933